SAGUARO'S GIFTS

By Kurt Cyrus and Illustrated by Andy Atkins

PUBLISHED by SLEEPING BEAR PRESS™

*Sleeping Bear Press wishes to thank Cam Juárez,
Community Engagement & Outreach Coordinator,
Saguaro National Park, for his careful reading and
review of the manuscript and art, and for offering
insightful feedback.*

SLEEPING BEAR PRESS™

Sleeping Bear Press
2395 South Huron Parkway, Suite 200
Ann Arbor, MI 48104
www.sleepingbearpress.com © Sleeping Bear Press

Printed and bound in the United States
10 9 8 7 6 5 4 3 2 1

Library of Congress Cataloging-in-Publication Data
Names: Cyrus, Kurt, author. | Atkins, Andy, 1958- illustrator.
Title: Saguaro's gifts / by Kurt Cyrus ; illustrated by Andy Atkins.
Description: Ann Arbor, MI : Sleeping Bear Press, [2021] |
Audience: Ages 4-8 | Summary: "In honor of its centenary, a majestic
cactus is celebrated by its neighbors, the local wildlife inhabitants, for
its gifts of food, shelter, and shade"— Provided by publisher.
Identifiers: LCCN 2021005308 | ISBN 9781534111301 (hardcover)
Subjects: LCSH: Saguaro—Juvenile literature. | Desert ecology—Juvenile literature.
Classification: LCC QK495.C11 C97 2021 | DDC 583.885—dc23
LC record available at https://lccn.loc.gov/2021005308

Among the spines, a *cactus flower* opens at the midnight hour.

The world is dark. The bloom is white.
A bat emerges from the night.

"Hello, Saguaro!

Every year I find the sweetest nectar here.

And happy birthday, by the way.
One hundred years, this very day!"

One hundred years of standing still
atop this rocky desert hill.
The starlight fades. The sky turns red.
A tiny owl comes home to bed.

"Hmmm . . ."

observes a hummingbird.
"I can't believe what I just heard.
One hundred years of keeping still?
I never could, and never will."

The nectar in the cactus bloom
invites a population boom
of butterflies and doves and bees.
"Go find another flower, please!"

Coyote grins from ear to ear.
"I thought I heard a party here.
A jolly romp, to say the least.
Am I invited to the feast?"

Rabbit whispers from her burrow:
"Happy hundredth, dear Saguaro.
Sorry that I had to run,
but say hello to everyone."

A tortoise lingers in the shade.
"My age is showing, I'm afraid.
But don't mind me. I only stopped
to see if any fruit has dropped."

Blossoms wither in the sun.
The pollination party's done.

Peck-peck-peck! "Pardon me,
I couldn't find a hollow tree.
We need a place to build a nest.
Of all the choices, you're the best."

"Peck away," the finches sing.
"You gouge a new hole every spring.
Is there an old one we can borrow?
Nothing beats a snug saguaro."

"Quiet!" snaps the sleepy owl. "This hole is mine, you prattling fowl.

Now hop away and let me sleep." "Cheep!" the finches answer. "Cheep!"

"Hey, Cactus!" says the porcupine.
"I can match you spine for spine,
but mine are barbed. You'll never see
a birdie pecking holes in me!"

All at once the pecking stops,
and caution grips the cactus tops.
Heads are bobbing all around.

Hold the chatter!
What's that sound?

A bobcat races up the trail
with javelina on his tail.
"Clear the way!" the bobcat screeches,
scrambling to the highest reaches.

Birds and lizards scatter quickly—

"*Eee! Ahh! Oooh!*"
This plant is prickly.

The javelina drift away.
The bobcat settles in to stay.

A lizard eats an orange ant.

"Happy birthday, big green plant."

Now the bobcat spreads his toes.
He picks a path, and down he goes.
It seems he's had a lot of practice
climbing barefoot on a cactus.

The tortoise creeps around the bend.

"Another day is done, old friend.
One hundred years have come and gone,
but you and I go on and on."

Saguaro's gifts are good and sweet:
a crop of tasty fruit to eat, some nectar for the thirsty bat, and refuge for a frightened cat.

In return, their gift to her
is pollination, swift and sure.
They eat the fruit and spread the seeds,
and this is all Saguaro needs.

The owl awakens in the night.
The cactus spreads its blooms of white.

The light from distant stars appears—
the journey of a thousand years.

Another gift exchange tomorrow—

Happy birthday, dear Saguaro.

Facts to Know about Saguaro

What makes a desert a desert? It's not the heat — there are cold deserts. It's not the sand, or the spiny plants. It's the lack of rain. Deserts are dry.

The saguaro (sah-WA-ro) cactus sends its roots out far and shallow, and then waits. Sometimes a few years may pass before a good rainfall comes. When it does finally happen, the cactus quickly takes up all the water it can hold, enough to last through a few more dry years if necessary.

This ability to store water makes the saguaro a sort of oasis in the desert. Animals gather in, on, and around the cactus. Bats, hummingbirds, doves, and insects come for the nectar and pollen in the cactus flowers. Many birds, including woodpeckers, owls, and finches, find shelter and nesting spots. All sorts of animals eat the ripe cactus fruit. And a few predators, such as the coyote and the bobcat, come to hunt.

Together they make a community where everyone benefits in one way or another, allowing life in the desert to go on.